An interview with

Anne Fine

EGMONT

Other authors in
the series:

Enid Blyton, Theresa Breslin,
Gillian Cross, Jamila Gavin, Michelle Magorian,
Michael Morpurgo, Jenny Nimmo,
Jacqueline Wilson, J.K. Rowling

Peter Hollindale began his career as a school teacher,
but has taught for many years at the University of York.
His work ranges from academic studies to an informal
reading guide for parents, *Choosing Books for Children*,
and he has published numerous articles and
reviews of children's books.

First published in Great Britain 1999 by Mammoth
This edition published 2002 by Egmont Books Limited,
239 Kensington High Street, London W8 6SA.

Interview questions, design and typesetting © 1999
Egmont Books Limited
Interview answers © 1999 Anne Fine
Anne's Books © 1999 Peter Hollindale
The Ship of Theseus © 2001 Anne Fine

ISBN 1 4052 0053 7

A CIP catalogue record for this title is available from the British Library.

Printed and bound in Great Britain
by Cox and Wyman Ltd, Reading, Berks.

Contents

Foreword

In 2001 Anne Fine was appointed the second Children's Laureate, taking over from the illustrator Quentin Blake. She holds the post for two years.

Anne is no stranger to honour and prizes. She won the coveted Carnegie Medal twice, for *Goggle Eyes* and *Flour Babies*, and has hoovered up all the other major prizes over the last few years, including the Smarties Prize, the Guardian Children's Fiction Award and the Whitbread Children's Novel Award. All this praise and recognition is for the writing she does quietly, at home, with just pencil and paper.

To be Children's Laureate is rather different. It isn't a reward for any single book, but recognition of all her stories – nearly fifty of them now – and the respect she has won from adults and children alike. And it isn't just an honour. It's a job.

For Anne's two years as Laureate she is a public figure. She gives talks, sits on committees and supports campaigns, all with one single purpose: helping children to discover and love books and reading. No one is better fitted to do that than Anne. As you read her interview, you will see how passionately she cares about reading and writing. In fact, some of the children in her stories are readers and writers themselves, including two in her most recent novels – bookworm Melanie in *Bad Dreams* and storyteller Ian in *Up On Cloud Nine*.

Anne has two particular ambitions for her period as Laureate. One is to help the cause of poetry for children. There are many fine poems that stay with you for life, if you read them first as a child. It is a shame to miss them. Anne hopes to promote poetry collections that will make the best-loved and the most memorable poems for children much more easily available to them.

Anne's other important project is the Home Library. Aiming to encourage a habit of reading, the Home Library scheme would distribute a new range of free, smart bookplates, and draw on all possible sources of books, enabling every child to collect and own a personal library. Nobody need be left out.

Anne in her job as Laureate is the same as Anne the writer: someone who invites children into the world of reading, and leaves no one out.

Peter Hollindale

Anne Fine is a distinguished writer for children of all ages, with over forty books to her credit. She is twice winner of the Carnegie Medal, Britain's most coveted children's literature award, and has also won the Guardian Children's Literature Award, the Whitbread Children's Novel Award twice, and a Smarties Prize. She won the Publishing News Children's Author of the Year Award in 1990 and again in 1993. An adaptation of her novel Goggle-Eyes has been shown by the BBC, and Twentieth Century Fox filmed her novel Madame Doubtfire as Mrs Doubtfire, starring Robin Williams. Her work has been translated into twenty-five languages.

www.annefine.co.uk

An interview with
Anne Fine
(by herself!)

My family and
my childhood

Tell me about your family.

There were quite a few of us. I'm the second of five sisters. I think my parents would have loved a son, so, after me, they tried one last time, and had triplet girls. We must have been a bit of a handful. The infant school next door took pity on my mother and let me in two years early. I can just remember pointing to letters and making the right noise – especially the tickly 'v' on my bottom lip. But other than that, I really can't remember a time when I couldn't read.

Did you enjoy that first school?

I don't remember how I felt, except that I know I hated the tepid milk we were forced to drink out of little glass bottles through horribly soggy paper straws. I don't recall much of the work we did, either, except the endless drawing of orbs and sceptres. For years I thought this was a normal part of the early school syllabus. I was amazed, for example, that neither of my own daughters had the faintest idea what an orb was, let alone how to draw one. Now, of course, I realise that I was at school through the Queen's coronation. And Empire Day, so I can draw a pretty nifty Union Jack, as well.

Anne centre stage as the Star of Bethlehem
in the school nativity play.

I always found learning words easy, so I tended to get quite large parts in the plays we put on each Christmas. One year I was the Star of Bethlehem, and told practically the whole story. The huge tinsel star on my back itched so fiercely that even today I cut the labels out of my clothes if I feel the least tickle.

Where were you living then?

In Fareham, in Hampshire. My father was an electrical engineer. He could fix anything, so though he had no great salary for those days and five children, we did have a car and used to go to pebbly south coast beaches. I still love the sea. We lived on one of the new council housing estates that were springing up all around. For years I thought the world smelled of sawdust and cement. Children were much freer then. Parents didn't feel the need to keep tabs on their whereabouts the way they do now. So we went 'exploring'. Orchards, alleys, woods, railway embankments, other people's gardens. We went round in little shifting gangs, and were tremendous trespassers – furtive rather than destructive. We only had to remember to come home at meal times, or when it began to get dark.

What about at home?

I spent hours making tiny little pretend books with scribble writing for all the dolls and soft toys. I had a Mobo – a sort of tin horse that went up and down – it may even have gone along a bit, I don't remember. And I had a scooter. (In a sentimental moment, I bought my daughters scooters, and wasn't *that* money down the drain; they clearly thought it was the lamest form of travel yet invented.) But books were my passion. At school, I was working my way through the spongy-covered Beacon Readers and out the other side to become what we so triumphantly called 'a free reader'.

* * *

My schooldays

What was your school like?

The junior school refused to take me till I was at least seven. So I stayed back a year, repeating some of the work, skipping the rest, and free to creep in and take any book I wanted out of the glass-fronted bookcase in the headteacher's office. Bliss!

Then I went on to primary school. We did everything: country dancing, nature walks, violin lessons, singing, sewing, swimming, more plays. (Once, helping to decorate the backcloth, I tipped over a whole bucket of paint.) And we had crazes: yo-yos, juggling, scrap books, stamp collecting, skipping, leapfrog, tiny silver derringer guns with noisy caps. My favourite teacher was Mr Simpson. He filled the classroom with smoke from his Kensitas Tipped cigarettes. (Back then, everyone in the world smoked everywhere. We all believed that air was yellow.) He played us records – Benjamin Britten's Young Person's Guide to the Orchestra, Tubby the Tuba, Peter and the Wolf – opening whole worlds. He read us *The Hobbit* ('Heads down, eyes closed!') and probably would have gone on to read us the whole of *The Lord of the Rings* if we hadn't had the big 'eleven plus' exam coming. I adored him. I still think of him with affection and gratitude.

Any lessons you hated?

Sewing. I'm what is called a 'bodger'. Even my plainly hemmed traycloth ended up grey and damp from being wept into, week after week. If ever I did manage to sew three or four stitches in a reasonably straight way, I'd find I'd also sewn them to my skirt, and I'd have to unpick them. Like Celeste in *The Angel of Nitshill Road*, I wasn't crazy about Maths. And I'm rubbish at Art. But, oh, how I hated sewing. I could barely breathe properly till the lesson was over.

Were you a nervous child generally?

I do think children were pounced on rather horribly in those days. Children now don't seem to go round expecting practically every adult they meet to tell them off for something. We did. If the headteacher appeared down the corridor, you'd tend to flatten yourself against the wall till he or she had gone by. I worried about all sorts of things. Nobody ever encouraged you to *explain*. And I bit my nails till they bled. (I still do.)

But bad times are useful for an author. When I was eight, we moved to a bigger house overlooking a graveyard. I was sure that my bedroom was haunted. Each night I saw a glowing skull shape on the wall. I'd call my parents, but as soon as they left, back it came. Of course, like all those hanged men that turn out to be your dressing gown on the back of the door, it proved to be something quite simple: the light from the landing shining through the keyhole on to the wall (blocked by my parents as they stood there saying, 'We can't see anything'). It made me miserable for months when I was young, but made a book, *The Haunting of Pip Parker*, when I remembered it years and years later.

Did you go to the library?

Did I go to the library? Do camels spit? I practically *lived* at the library. All writers do. Back then, the rule was: Only Two Books At Once. I had real problems with one librarian, who used to peer suspiciously at the books I brought back and say, 'You only took these out two days ago.' I'd shuffle about a bit and tell her, 'But I have read them.' And she'd smile nastily and thrust them back at me over the counter. 'Well, you can't have read them properly, so take them back and read them again.'

You'd never find someone with that attitude in a library now.

What were your favourite books?

I wish I could say *Mistress Masham's Repose*, by T.H. White, because, along with his masterpiece, *The Once and Future King*, I think it's one of the most enjoyable, and richest, of reads for a bright child. But I didn't come across it till I was 25.

So, Enid Blyton, up through *The Magic Faraway Tree* (my very favourite) through *The Famous Five*, and *The Castle* (and *River*, and *Mountain*, and everything else) *of Adventure* series. I had no time at all for *The Secret Seven*. I couldn't be doing with them.

As I grew older I had a passion for Anthony Buckeridge's *Jennings* books, and longed to go to boarding school (preferably a boys' one, like his). But my most treasured children's author was Richmal Crompton. (I still remember my amazement when I was told she was a woman.) I've kept all my *William* books. They're battered and chewed, and dunked in the bath, but they still have pride of place on my bookshelves. I loved William. He was my imaginary companion for years.

I missed a lot of the classics. I didn't meet A.A. Milne's *Winnie the Pooh* or Beatrix Potter's *Peter Rabbit* till

I read them to my own children. But I did have *Alice in Wonderland* (though I much preferred Carroll's *Through the Looking Glass*), and I read *The Secret Garden* by Frances Hodgson Burnett. I missed the Nesbit books till I was grown up, too. It's such a shame not to get to read the right book for the first time ever at the right age. Another vital reason for the whole family to live at the library!

Did you read poetry?

Not on my own, no. But in secondary school I took something called 'Extra Speech', for which we had to learn a poem a week, so, over the years, I learned a tremendous amount of poetry by heart. I'm glad I did. I love the way patches of verse I barely understood at the time rise up to colour certain moments. Once, on a visit to Shetland, I found myself pacing along a rugged path in foul northern weather, watching waves smash the cliff, and suddenly I realised I was singing a song into the gale at the top of my voice – a song we'd learned by heart in primary school when I was eight.

Wha'll buy my caller herrin'?

They're bonnie fish and halesome farin';

Wha'll buy my caller herrin'?

New drawn frae the Forth.

When ye were sleepin' on your pillows,

Dream'd ye aught o' oor puir fellows,

Darkling as they faced the billows,

A' to fill our woven willows –

What I found amazing was that, when we learned to sing it, I had not the faintest idea what any of the song meant. The Scots dialect was never explained, and for all it meant to us, it might just as well have been written in Serbo-Croat. I think I probably recognised the word 'herring' in the first verse. Probably. And in the second, the phrase 'sleepin' on your pillows' must have conjured up some sort of image. But as for all the rest, it was a perfect mystery. *Halesome farin'? Frae the Forth? Darkling?*

And now here I was, years and years later, bellowing it out, still word-perfect, and having for the first time a sense of the song's real beauty and power. The guilt-inducing cry of the fisherwoman. 'Buy it! It's good for you! And our men risked their lives to get it here. So buy it!' I suppose understanding, like pills, as often as not comes with timed release.

I don't think I could write a poem unless I needed it for a novel. In *Flour Babies*, I couldn't think of the perfect song Simon's father might have been singing when he left home. So I wrote a sea shanty. And I wrote several of the patches of verse in *Charm School*. But I wouldn't exactly call them poetry . . .

Tell me about your earliest writing.

That was in primary school. It was wonderful. We never had to discuss things, or toss ideas about first. The teacher would just put four or five titles up on the board and tell us to choose one, shut up and get on with it. If you finished too early, you just had to sit quietly and twiddle your thumbs till the bell rang. If you didn't finish in time, bad luck, because you'd lose marks for not having a proper ending. (All our work was marked. Spellings and punctuation were corrected. You had to copy spellings out three times, unless they were shamefully easy mistakes, in which case you had to write them out ten times.)

We wrote these 'compositions' over two lessons, in silence. It was the best possible practice for learning to 'pace' a story properly with a beginning, middle and end. Far better (and far less boring) than the ghastly 'drafting and redrafting' my poor children suffered. I expect there were people who hated it. But it was ideal for someone like me who just wanted to pick up her pencil, shut out the world, and fly.

So did you think you might become an author?

It never occurred to me. I think I thought books were born on the library shelves.

What did you want to be?

Nothing. I never really believed I ever would truly be an adult doing a job, earning a living. Adults kept asking, 'What do you want to be when you grow up?' I'd give what I somehow had picked up was 'the right answer' for a girl in those days. 'I want to be a teacher or a librarian. Or maybe a physiotherapist.' Though I had simply no idea what a physiotherapist was, or did.

* * *

My career

What did you do between school and becoming a full-time writer?

I had the oddest series of jobs. I'd studied Spanish, French and History in the sixth form, and History and Politics at University.

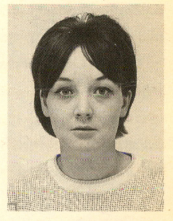

Anne at university.

(I suspect that's part of the reason that I'm so interested in social issues.) I had a job more or less lined up in London, but then I fell in love and married someone whose job was near Coventry. So first I taught for a year at a girls' secondary school. I don't think I've envied a teacher since!

Then I became the secretary of a County Public Health Officer. That job had its moments. Irate people would post in letters with pineapple chunks pinned to the top left-hand corner. 'Inside this chunk, you will see there is a dead beetle. When I buy tinned fruit, I scarcely expect . . . bleh, bleh, bleh.' Once, some distraught woman brought in a milk bottle that had a strange grey shadow against the glass at the bottom. It was a dead mouse, and she'd already drunk half the milk before she noticed it.

Then I was an assistant in Oxfam's information office, writing up reports on many of their projects overseas. That job changed my view of the world, and my priorities, forever. Then we moved north, to Edinburgh. My last job was teaching in a prison.

* * *

My career as a writer

How did you come to write your very first book?

I was 24, and stuck in a cold top flat with my first baby daughter. Only the almost daily trips to the library were keeping me sane. And then there was a blizzard.

Edinburgh is all hills, the pavements weren't gritted, and we couldn't afford sitters. So I was trapped inside with nothing fresh to read, and after a few hours I must have gone spare enough to snatch up a pencil and start to write. It was a novel called *The Summer House Loon*, a very gentle and light book, set in a glorious garden on one summer's day and night.

There are a good many gardens in your writing. What's the reason for that?

I was so lucky. When I was nine, we had moved to a large, slightly tumbledown old house in a village in Northamptonshire. It had a beautiful garden with high walls all around. I spent hours on the walls, on the lawn, up the trees, reading and eating green apples and unripe rhubarb. (In my family, if you tried waiting till fruit was ripe, one or another of your sisters would already have eaten it.) I think gardens symbolise for me a protected past, time out of mind.

Landscape – countryside – they're important, too. Both my best friends at school lived even deeper in the country than I did. We spent whole days exploring, walking miles, mucking about. I still need to be in green places every day. That's why we've always had a dog: first, Ben, our soft and stupid labrador retriever, and now Henry, a huge, hairy Bernese mountain dog. They certainly make you walk.

Henry, the Burnese mountain dog.

You have a dog. But there's some suspicion that you're not crazy about cats. Is this an evil rumour, or the truth?

I hated our cats. With me, they were snotty and unco-operative. However, my daughter Cordelia adored them, and they spent most of their lives asleep on her pillows or draped round her neck purring away like engines. And in the garden, of course, stalking poor hapless fledglings, like Tuffy in

Anne's daughter, Cordelia, with the cat.

Diary of a Killer Cat. Though I find the thought of that less horrible than the thought of animals stuck in cages. That's why I wrote *Countdown*, to make people *think* before they pestered their parents for a gerbil. And like Mum in *Crummy Mummy and Me*, and my enchanting Flora in *The Stone Menagerie*, I think zoos, for large sentient creatures, are things you could simply not invent now. People would be disgusted by the very idea.

Let's get on to the nitty gritty of writing. How do you actually do it?

With a soft 2B pencil. It's easier to rub out.

I've nothing against machines (though I've yet to see anyone's writing improved by one: indeed, I think authors have a natural speed of working and they get faster at their peril).

I'm a slow worker. I pore over each sentence, rubbing out and rewriting over and over. So I get grubby, covered in those claggy rubber droppings. I work on a few pages at a time. A chapter will have to be pretty well worked out down to the last comma before I'll move on to the next. I write a bit, then try to come at it as a reader, over and over, as if it were fresh. Would it make sense to me? Would I want to know more about this first? Would I be bored? So much of the skill involved is in the *reading* rather than the writing. That's why the advice of many of the best writers to children who want to be authors is, 'Don't worry about the writing yet. Just read, read, read. Because only if you're

The author at work.

a *reader* will you know whether it's working, and, if not, how to fix it so it does.' And reading's like any other skill. You have to put in the hours. That's why I'm always batting on and on about libraries. *Nobody's* parents have both the time *and* the money to furnish them with all the books they need.

I work in absolute silence, apart from my own mutterings. I type up sections on my ancient typewriter and suddenly it looks different, more like a book, and I'll start nit-picking all over again. At school, I hated corrections more than anything. I just loathed going back to things. If you had told me I would end up spending my days the way I do now, I simply would not have believed you. Now, for some mysterious reason, I find spending whole years on things, getting them absolutely right, both satisfying and soothing. I love my work. To me, it's like that moment in a noisy swimming pool when you first slip under the water, and all that din and thrashing round you vanishes, leaving you alone with yourself in a silent world. I think I'd go mad if I couldn't write.

How long does a book take?

Novels for older children can take about a year. Books for much younger children are always shorter and simpler, and much, much quicker. Once you've had the idea, it might take only a couple of months to write something like *Design a Pram*, or *Countdown*. The middle range of books, like *The Angel of Nitshill Road*, *The Chicken Gave It to Me*, or *Bill's New Frock* usually have a good deal more thinking behind them than the younger books, because it's possible to go so much deeper into things that matter. So they take months – almost as long as the books for older readers. One adult novel I wrote took me over two years, on and off. It nearly killed me.

Tell me about your work day.

Because I started to write when I had young children, I very quickly got in the habit of rushing back to whichever novel I was working on the moment they fell asleep, or went to nursery. It was miles easier when they started school. Whole hours of peace! Then, publishers never seemed to phone, and I gave almost no talks. Now, it's a rare day without an interruption. The explosion of interest in the author, rather than the book, has put a huge burden on writers who weren't fortunate enough to have earned their reputations before all this travel and publicity work became part of the job.

So something has to give. In my case, it's tidiness and shopping. I wouldn't win any Natty Housekeeping awards. And I shop as rarely as possible, and very fast, and only for essentials like food, or replacements for things that are broken. I wear my clothes practically till they fall off me. I see these people standing still on shop escalators and I think, 'Isn't there anything they want to be doing more than being in here?' Once, in Australia, at a big theatre event, a little boy came to the microphone and asked, 'My mother wants to know,

Anne being interviewed for a school magazine.

how do you do it?' And the answer came out, just flew out: 'I don't shop.'

Ideally, I wake around seven and read the papers in bed with my tea. Then I walk the dog and have breakfast. I'm not surprised studies show people who don't eat breakfast work at fifteen percent less capacity. I can't work at all if I haven't eaten. First, I clear urgent mail and faxes. Then I try to get to my own stuff. I eat lunch at my desk. (My paperwork ends up quite colourful: avocado, humus, mayonnaise, tomato . . .) Around four, I'll often feel tired, and knock off, maybe go and have a long read in the bath, walk the dog again, start on the endless other stuff still glowering at me from the in-tray: requests, invitations, letters, proofs, decisions, invoices, travel arrangements. That could take hours more. I always admire authors who just ignore all that. I just can't bring myself to hurl it all in the bin, but I'm often tempted. I do let it pile up if I'm close to the end of a book. Once an avalanche fell on me, so I have two in-trays now.

Where do you work?

Wherever. I used to write at the kitchen table. Then I used the dining room and cleared it if we had guests. For the last seven years I've worked in a corner of the bedroom, overlooking a patch of common land and the river, and lots of sky. As long as it's quiet, I can work anywhere.

Do you believe some people are born storytellers?

I think I do. Take my Granny Bertha. Not only was every story she told wonderful, convoluted, filled with drama and emotional interest, but you could see in her the mind of the storyteller in action.

Sent up to wash your hands before the meal, you

might catch the basis of the story, almost the plain, unvarnished truth. 'I've just been in the post office and that Mrs Sharp gave me a very funny look.' By the time the table had been laid, the story would have taken root and sprouted its first shoots. 'I just popped my head round the door, no more than that, and the *look* she gave me! Honestly! That woman could crack stone. They ought to chain her up in the quarry! They wouldn't need any more of their machines!' Over lunch, she'd fill in a bit of the background and emotional development. 'She's *always* hated me, of course. It's because of my George. Mind you, you can't blame her. Stuck with that Henry, what woman wouldn't go peculiar? There's something very strange about her Henry . . .' Dialogue would be added gradually. 'So I said, "Is there a problem, Mrs Sharp?" She went red as a turkeycock. I've never seen a body change colour so fast. You could have cooked these chops on her, Mary, honestly you could.'

Through the long, rainy afternoon, we'd hear the story a dozen times or more. The short exchange would burgeon, gloriously and mysteriously, into a fifteen or twenty minute tale of envy and bitterness, hostile challenges and viper-tongued replies. By teatime, a whole supporting cast would have been added. 'So I turned to that Mr Bruce from the Co-op –' 'I thought you told us there was no one else there.' 'I never said that. You can't have been listening properly. No, I turned to Mr Bruce and I said, ever so frostily –' 'Upstairs, you children. It's well past your bedtime.' 'But we're listening. We're listening to Granny.' 'You've heard it all before.' 'But it was different then.' 'I don't care. Granny's telling Daddy now. Off you all go to bed.'

And so my father got the best of it. The final, tirelessly crafted, beautifully polished story. And it was wasted on him, wasted utterly, because the fact that it was not the *truth* (nothing *like*: truth had been left standing several hours ago) bothered him and ruined his enjoyment of the story. But me, I'd be hovering at the bottom of the stairs, contentedly eavesdropping, unwittingly learning my future trade – the storyteller's apprentice.

But all of your books are very different. Where do you get your ideas?

Everywhere. You learn to recognise what sort of thing

can make a story, or fit in a book. You find yourself thinking, 'I can use that,' and making a note on a piece of paper. I even have a file of scrappy messages to myself, some now totally incomprehensible even to me, called 'Things to Use Later'.

Often, I think, 'What if . . .?' What if people came to our planet and wanted to eat us roasted and fried and baked? (*The Chicken Gave It to Me*). Sometimes you take a state of affairs you see next door, or on television, or even in your own family, and you throw in a 'What if . . .?' to ratchet it up a bit. Like, new stepmother, but what if they *hated* her? Story!

Sometimes, I simply pinch ideas from newspapers. *Diary of a Killer Cat* came from an article on the new stories we hear all around us. You know. 'My friend's friend knows someone who . . .' They're called urban myths. *Design a Pram* came from an article about the way girls and boys respond so differently to set tasks: designing a pram was the example given. The girls made cosy, safe ones; the boys made ones that went at high speeds and were radio-controlled so the parent could stay home. All I usually have to do is find 'the voice' of the story. Or the point of view. Or where in the story it's best to start and finish.

I write the older books, and the adult books, because something's bothering me and I want to work out how I feel about it and where I stand. With *Goggle-Eyes* and *Madame Doubtfire*, I was obviously thinking about the effects of divorce and remarriage on children. I had a lot of letters from children claiming, from bitter experience, that the happy ending in *Goggle-Eyes* was, as they so often put it, 'a cop-out'. So I wrote *Step by Wicked Step* to think about second families. I think one of the most valuable things an author can do is show people how very complicated life is.

As in 'The Tulip Touch'?

Oh, yes. A lot of authors wrote about horrible things that year. The newspapers had been full of stories about ghastly things done by really quite young children. I wasn't the only one who needed to think about it – and its effects on other children reading those same papers. It's not important, though, always to find the answer. It *is* important to think about things in greater depth. People who can't do that lead impoverished lives, they really do. And books are the best way of learning how people tick. They are also the best way of thinking about how we ought to live.

Reading 'Bill's New Frock' in braille at the National Library for the Blind, Stockport.

Can't television do that just as well?

Absolutely not. Telly can show you, absolutely brilliantly, what happened next. It can't begin to tell you why, or how people struggled with their conscience, or what in their deep past made them act that way, or how they really felt about it afterwards. Only the author can do that. Even on soaps, all you'll learn is what people *think* they think, what they *think* they feel. The book can go far, far deeper.

Is that why you write?

I'd like to think I write just to provide 'a good read' – enchantment, pleasure, escape – because that's why I myself read. But I do think that there is so often this enriching fall-out from reading that it's mad not to praise reading for its 'added value'.

And though some telly is excellent, vast swathes of

it are simply a massive and addictive waste of time for children. You see them sitting through hours of drivel that even they are bored by, waiting for the one person who's been trailered they really want to see. I have to admit I was *ruthless* with my own children. Downright cruel. 'Turn off that telly. You're only watching rubbish.' It was well worth it. They're *brilliant* readers – much better than I was at their age.

Do you read reviews of your work?

Oh, yes. I read them. A lot of them are really cheering. You think, at least *someone* understands what I was trying to do. I suspect that bad reviews only really hurt when, deep inside, the author knows the criticism is just. If it's just nonsense, or spite, you could dismiss it far more easily.

A nosy question. Do you put your family in your books?

I certainly wouldn't tell you if I did! But, sometimes, I'll admit, I do put in bits of them, though I suspect I put myself in more – usually exasperated. I swear I'm the bad-tempered genie in *A Sudden Puff of Glittering Smoke*.

It's based on my impatience with how little my children seemed to be taught at school about other times and other places.

But people are so complicated. They're so subtle. They're like those mirrored disco balls, they have hundreds of facets, and only a great novelist could fit in more than a very few. Sometimes you keep a side of someone's character, but change their age, or sex. But Jan Mark said it best. 'Writers don't write about people they know. They write what they know about people.'

What do your children think about your books?

I *never* speak for my children. And I try not to talk about them, either. I think it must be the worst thing, having a writer for a parent. Everyone needs privacy in which to grow. Bad enough having people guessing which bits of which books might mirror real life, without pitching in to give clues.

But do you write for children because of your own?

No. I write for children because I enjoy it, I can do it,

and children are the best readers. They never say to you things like, 'Oh, I started it but I've been far too busy to finish it.' If they like it, they read through all that please-will-you-put-that-book-down-and-lay-the-table nagging, to the end. I know that, as a child, I was an author's perfect reader – absolutely committed, passionate and grateful. I write for those readers, just as earlier writers wrote for children like me.

Which do you prefer, writing for adults or children?

Neither. But they are very different. With children, you have to take great care to be accessible. And you mustn't overestimate their knowledge or underestimate their intelligence. With adults, you can just fly, and if they can't follow you, or don't want to, that's up to them.

What do you like best about the job?

The silence. I love that.

Not having to *share*. At school, the words I dreaded most were 'Now choose a partner'. I like being totally in control of what I do. That's why I've never got involved in writing for film or television.

And I love the sheer *addictiveness* of the job. Out of nowhere – just seeing or hearing, or even thinking, something – you feel a sort of nudge inside your brain, and it's, 'Oh, right. So that's what I'm going to write about next.' Then it's as if you grow some sort of special antennae. Everything seems to feed into what you're thinking about. Things you wouldn't even have noticed before turn into grist for your mill.

Then, mad as this sounds, it's almost as if, somewhere, the book's already written and you simply have to find it. You try it this way. No. You try it that. Maybe start earlier in the story. Or from a different point of view, perhaps with 'he' or 'she', and not 'I' telling the story. And, like brushing sand off ancient stones to see what lies beneath, you somehow gradually find the book, as if it had been lying waiting for you all along.

Do you get stuck?

Oh, yes. I get stuck. Often it's hard to know whether to step back and take a break and come at it fresh another time, or just press on. Because you have to take your own moods into account a bit. Sometimes you come downstairs thinking, 'This is one of the best things I've ever written', and the very next day you can be thinking, 'This is real garbage. Utter drivel. Best to put it in the bin.' The philosopher Bertrand Russell said that nothing you write is ever as bad as you fear or as good as you hope. That's comforting. And, if you're patient, you generally come to know fairly definitely whether it is better to rip it up, or press on.

What do you hate most about the job?

If I'm honest, probably the growing obsession with covers. I especially dislike coming across people who act as if the covers are practically as important as the words. They're not, so it's stupid to act that way. It breaks my heart to hear people who have half a brain, and should know better, admitting they haven't bothered with a book because of its cover, or because the cover wasn't right for the boys, or whatever. So rip it off. Or get the library helpers to paste something better over it. But don't not get it. Don't not *read* it. And I get exasperated when I travel for hours to give talks, then the first question is what do I think about this or that cover. Left to myself, I wouldn't give a flying crumpet about covers. That's not how bright people choose their books, after all, is it?

What do you read?

A lot of fiction. Autobiographies and biographies. Psychology. Stuck in a lift, *anything*.

Do you like theatre?

Not very much. I find the sheer falseness of it grates on me. But that is odd, since I love cinema and opera, and you could argue that they're even more that way.

Who do you admire most?

No contest! My hero is Andrew Carnegie, the great philanthropist who funded so many of our public libraries. There was a marble statue of him in my home town library. He's definitely the only man with a beard I would ever have considered marrying.

Your favourite words?

Silver. Captain. Frangipani. Galleon. All words to

conjure with. I suppose if a Captain stepped off a silver galleon and offered me some frangipani, I'd be lost. (Frangipani, for those who have lost their dictionaries, is a scented plant.)

Andrew Carnegie

Your favourite characters in your own books?

Chester Howard. Celeste. Ally in *The Stone Menagerie*. Iolanthe in *Jennifer's Diary*. And Will in *The Book of the Banshee*.

What do you do in your spare time?

I read. I paint walls different colours. I love doing that. I walk the dog more. I go to the cinema. I sit on the steps in the garden, and tell Dick, my partner, how he ought to be doing things differently.

What would you like to have been if you couldn't be an author?

If I could do anything? *Anything*? Then I'd sing opera.

That would be glorious. Sadly, I'm a very poor singer – one of those people they say can't carry a tune in a bag. So it's just as well for everyone I don't have the choice.

But I get the feeling books seem more real to you than living. Is this true?

It certainly *feels* that way. But I know from long experience that if I'm worried about one of my daughters, say, or really upset about something, then I can't work. So it can't be true really.

Of what are you proudest?

My daughters, giving up smoking and my two Carnegie Medals.

You've written a lot of books, won a lot of prizes. Are you at all surprised at how your life's turned out?

When I was at school, one of the teachers gave us careers advice. 'Find out what you like doing most in all the world, and then find someone who'll pay you to do it.' I feel so privileged. It's not everyone who gets the chance to spend their life, as in a fairy tale, trying to spin the plain old straw of everyday life into pure gold.

Anthony Browne, with his Kate Greenaway Medal for 'Zoo';
Michael Palin; Anne Fine with her Carnegie Medal
for 'Flour Babies', in 1992.

Anne's Books

An overview by
Peter Hollindale

Anne Fine's books for children are comedies of growing-up, with the underlying seriousness that all good comedy has. The hallmark of her work is acceptance. Never condescending or indulgent, she nevertheless takes people as they are, both child and adult, and finds a place for everyone. In Anne's work, eccentricity is not abnormality but a fact of life. It is a world that her readers, young and old, find gratefully familiar.

The madness of life

In his celebrated novel *A High Wind in Jamaica*, about the relationship between a group of children and the pirates who have accidentally kidnapped them, Richard Hughes set out his views on children: 'Agreed that their minds are not just more ignorant and stupider than ours, but differ in kind of thinking (are *mad*, in fact); but one can, by an effort of will and imagination, think like a child.' Anne would certainly not agree that children are mad. In her work for adults, such as her novel *The Killjoy* and her radio play *The Captain's Court Case*, she has written about genuine madness and psychopathic ruthlessness. But her 'effort of will and imagination' has brilliantly illuminated the comic equivalents of madness which constantly arise in daily transactions between adults and the young.

Occasions of mild lunacy are everywhere in Anne's children's books. Even the word 'psychopath' appears, though jokily used about a non-human character. Ellie's father in *The Diary of a Killer Cat* refers to Tuffy the cat – whose anti-social habit is to haul his prey through the cat-flap and mess up carpets with it – as "you great fat furry psychopath". But only once in the children's books does ordinary, everyday, growing-up lunacy shade into something altogether darker and more sinister – in her recent novel *The Tulip Touch*, which stands apart from the rest of her work. Otherwise she creates unerring true-to-life comedy from the 'madness' that Richard Hughes noticed – the 'madness' of children and adolescents as adults see them, along with the reciprocal madness of adults from the point of view of children. And because children live in families, whether broken or unbroken, and are obliged to go to schools, they spend much of their lives in intimate contact with grown-ups. Life is one long comedy of negotiation and affectionate war between two sets of people who are each, from the other's stand-point, frequently stark staring mad. At least, it is a comedy when viewed from the outside, but not always very funny from within.

Playing fair

Anne's great strength as a children's novelist is that she shows both the outside and the inside, both the hilarious external farce of home and school and the often painful reality of first-hand experience. Moreover, she plays scrupulously fair. There are children's writers who side unashamedly with the child's viewpoint, forming an authorial conspiracy with the child against the adult world. This is not Anne's way at all. When adults behave 'unreasonably', as they often do, there is actually a reason for it, even though the reason may be physical or emotional rather than strictly rational (just like children's own 'unreasonable' behaviour, in fact). Already in Anne's second book, *The Other, Darker Ned*, this careful balance is apparent. The heroine, Ione Muffet, is organising a jumble sale for Oxfam, and tours her village in search of sites for her posters. An obvious target is the village grocer, Mr Heath, usually a friendly character. She catches him in a bad mood, and he refuses outright to accept a poster: "They cut out the light." This is not his real reason. His baby son Geoffrey is 'grizzling softly' in the crook of his arm.

Mr Heath . . . had had a very bad day.

Geoffrey had kept him up all the night before with his crying, and was probably going to do the same thing tonight. And Mr Heath had a headache. He didn't quite know why he was picking an argument with Ione. All he wanted was for her to go away and leave him in peace, taking her poster with her.

This early book is the shape of things to come for Anne's work. It is the sequel to *The Summer House Loon*, and shares a central cast of Ione herself, who is in early adolescence, her blind father, a professor of history, and a young couple – Ned Hump, a history student, and her father's secretary Caroline, who share a tempestuous love affair and marriage. But the two books are very different. *The Summer House Loon* is a quite sophisticated comedy, in which the youthful Ione is a spectator and benevolent meddler in the academic and romantic follies of the grown-ups. In *The Other, Darker Ned* she seems both younger and older, more wayward and more actively self-assertive, even downright rude, as she is to the unfortunate Mr Heath. Yet her misdeeds are all in a very good cause, with the warm-hearted (but hot-headed!) idealism of adolescence.

Anne's heroes and heroines

Although Ione is completely individual, she is also the prototype for a series of Anne Fine heroes and heroines. There are common denominators in late childhood and the teenage years which are regularly captured in Anne's longer books with sharp accuracy and wit: the struggle towards personal identity; the impatient diagnosis of parental weaknesses, especially when one of them is available for weekend access only or is missing altogether; the mixture of solicitous love for these parents with real need for emotional support; the capacity under pressure to be more grown-up than the grown-ups; the sibling loyalties and conflicts; the constant heady sense of life on the move. Kitty Killin in *Goggle-Eyes*, Will and Estelle in *The Book of the Banshee*, Simon Martin in *Flour Babies*, Tom and Cass in *Round Behind the Ice-House*, a quintet of children from broken homes in *Step by Wicked Step*, and even the very special case of Natalie in *The Tulip Touch*, are caught up in the turmoil of personal growth and family tensions, and we can see the things they have in common. Even the gender divide, though clearly marked, is not clear-cut. Boys and girls are different sexes but not, as in some writers, different species. And whatever they share as the general truths of childhood and adolescence, they are never clones but always sharply individualised.

As this brief sketch of the adolescent scenario makes clear, Anne's books are typically versions of the 'problem novel'. They are intended both to entertain and, when they meet the right reader who needs it, to help. She makes the point explicitly in a passage at the end of *Goggle-Eyes*, though it is neatly off-loaded by the child narrator on to an English teacher, Mrs Lupey:

> *It's one of Loopy's Great Theories. She's always on about it. Living your life is a long and doggy business, says Mrs Lupey. And*

stories and books help. Some help you with the living itself. Some help you just take a break. The best do both at the same time.

If school and home are the childhood settings for this 'long and doggy business', Anne tends to reserve school for her books aimed at 'younger' and 'middle range' readers. For very young children, she seems to imply, the school is a major centre for amusement and anxiety and drama, while home is reasonably dependable and placid. (And it might be unwise to plant anxieties about the home where none exist.) For older readers the emphasis is reversed. Although school figures marginally in most of the longer books for older readers, it is not usually a source of major stress. In this group only *Flour Babies* is firmly school-centred. Home is where the action is.

Relationships

At home there are three generations to provide potential battlegrounds – siblings, parents and step-parents, and the old – though only *The*

Granny Project actively involves all three at once. For the youngest readers there are also pets. Across the books there is a wide range of sibling relationships. The 'babies' of the family, parental afterthoughts, are treated protectively by their elders. Lydia in *Madame Doubtfire* rebukes her childishly histrionic father for his extravagant mime of cutting their mother's throat: ' "Oh, do stop being so silly!" Lydia scolded her father impatiently. "You're almost making Natty cry." ' However, there is also a parental role for older children when parents themselves fall down on it, and Lydia at once turns her guns the other way: "Now just stop being so wet, Natty." Will Flowers in *The Book of the Banshee* is similarly protective of his baby sister Muffy during times of family stress. Like Lydia, though, he can be a more effective parent than the parents. Muffy refuses to talk and is a pre-school educational worry, until Will, with loving toughness, cracks the problem.

At a different stage there can be sibling jealousy. Not the least of Natalie's problems in *The Tulip Touch* is the constant realisation that her younger brother Julius is her mother's favourite. At one point she makes clear and cynical use of the fact to get her own way. But sibling wars are at their most explosive when boy and girl are teenagers together. Anne's most radical treatment of the situation comes in *Round Behind the Ice-House*, which (*The Tulip Touch* excepted) is her most serious book to date – serious, at any rate, in the conspicuous absence of the comedy which elsewhere offsets some painful themes. Tom and Cass are twins, and have been friends and allies throughout a stern and solitary farming childhood. Adolescence breaks all that. Cass's mind is more vivacious than Tom's at any time, but he is finally dispossessed of his sister by that spurt of mental and emotional growth which causes adolescent girls to leave the boys behind. *Round Behind the Ice-House* is the sinister tale of the ordeal which brings Tom his hard-won confidence and individual identity. *The Book of the Banshee* plays out the same rite of passage, as Will's sister Estelle – another good sibling friend in earlier childhood – inflicts her adolescence on the family, but this time the results are hilarious as well as emotionally true.

When siblings gang up instead of fighting, they can be a formidable force. This happens in *Madame Doubtfire*, which in some respects is Anne's most daring book. Lydia, Christopher and Natalie go to and fro between their divorced parents, the victims of endless petty disputes over access. In this novel it is clearly the parents who are 'mad'. The book is daring because it violates the adult gender stereotypes so sharply. The children's mother, Miranda Hilliard, is a successful businesswoman, Managing Director of Hilliard's Lighting Emporium, and almost a cliché of 'male' authority and efficiency. Their father, Daniel, by contrast, is an actor who is usually out of work and whose best-remembered professional talent, for cross-dressing, he now turns to good account by masquerading as a female housekeeper to gain extra access to the children. It makes a change from his recent work in nude modelling. Nowhere else in Anne's books are gender expectations so flagrantly inverted. But so, in effect, are the roles of adult and child. Never shown as artificially mature, the children under pressure are nevertheless more sensible, discreet, cunning and far-sighted than their parents.

More difficult themes

An altogether more complicated case is that of the four siblings in *The Granny Project*. In an earlier book, *The Stone Menagerie*, Anne first tackled the delicate subject of a child's encounter with adult mental illness. In that book, Ally is sentenced to endure repeated Sunday visits to the psychiatric hospital where silent Aunt Chloe is confined. One weekend he makes an independent visit and through various comic misadventures brings about an accidental therapy. It is a difficult theme for comedy. The author treads minefields of sensitivity and taste. In *The Granny Project* the same essential theme is carried further, and triumphantly so. No therapy can come to Granny's aid. She is old and senile. When the sibling quartet discover their parents' plan to put Granny in a Home, they devise a set of counter-moves of ferocious subtlety to thwart them. The book is very funny, not least at moments when we see the family from the outside observer's viewpoint, as we do on Granny's disastrous visit to the polling booth. But under the laughter there is a bedrock of painful and universal human dilemmas and truths. As so often, the comic, banal and trivial surface of home and school is thin but necessary ice, covering depths of intractable emotion.

Comedy is perhaps less effective in the much-praised *Flour Babies*, which won the Carnegie Medal and Whitbread Award. Simon is a difficult teenager. His father walked out on his mother, casually whistling, when Simon was only a few weeks old. Living with this awkward mystery, Simon learns through an improbable school project that he himself can be a good father – provided he waits long enough and enjoys his independence first. This is the only time in Anne's work where the unexceptionable message seems to dictate the novel, and the book's warm reception seems prompted by the message rather than the story.

The Tulip Touch, on the other hand, is a masterpiece. Born from a climate of public hysteria about instances of so-called 'evil' child behaviour, it tackles head-on the question of whether children can be born evil. Natalie's mother thinks they can. "Tulip is downright *evil*." Her father thinks not. "No one is born evil. No one. And especially not Tulip." The reader must decide about poor, violent, cruel, fire-raising, solitary, beaten, abused Tulip. For years she is Natalie's best and only friend, and it is Natalie the complex storyteller – Natalie from a seemingly good home, with seemingly good parents, Natalie the privileged survivor – who confronts us most starkly with the crassness of our urge and need to pigeonhole Tulip as evil, and thereby victimise a victim. There are messages here, too, and deeply important ones, but to understand them we must bring our own imagination to the story.

Seeing through someone else's eyes

Imagination is itself a theme in Anne's work for

middle-range and younger readers. These short books touch more lightly on serious themes than the longer stories, but by no means ignore them. In *Jennifer's Diary*, the young Iolanthe, a compulsive storyteller, covets the brand-new diary which belongs to unimaginative Jennifer, whose writing powers stretch only to 'Jan 1st. It was quite cold today.' Iolanthe can do much better than that, and invades the tempting book with stories of her own, but realises in the process that even the most exuberant storytellers need diplomacy and tact. The most important of imaginative gifts, after all, is to put yourself in someone else's place and see life through their eyes.

This is the underlying serious theme in many of Anne's short books for the very young. It is a gift you need quite early in life, and books can help. Like Iolanthe, several other heroes and heroines are shown acquiring it at school. In the deservedly famous *Bill's New Frock*, Bill suffers a sartorial sex-change for just one school day. Sent off to school in a pink frock, he learns some salutary lessons about the different expectations placed by peers and teachers on the sexes. Some work in favour of girls: Bill in his frock is gently ushered into school by the headmaster on sentry duty, while the boys are harried and hectored. But usually the balance tilts the other way, as Bill finds out when he impedes the boys' football game at breaktime. Always a comedy, never a lesson, *Bill's New Frock* is a seductive first encounter with the politics of gender!

Louis in *Loudmouth Louis* also learns to see himself as others see him. An irrepressible talker, he discovers through a sponsored silence how much better life is for his friends, and for himself, when his constant chatter is turned off. In *How To Write Really Badly*, a rather longer book for middle-range readers, cheerfully opinionated Chester Howard – a very modern, cosmopolitan boy with a working mother and a houseperson father – is shaken by the unnerving niceness of his new school. But he – and the school, the teacher, and the reader – learn an important lesson when his deskmate, hopeless and illiterate Joe Gardener, proves to have a secret genius for imaginative modelling. Talent and imagination have their own 'laws': never write anyone off.

The Angel of Nitshill Road is probably Anne's best school story for the middle range. With a very serious theme – the cruelty of bullying, the typecasting of children, and the lazy connivance of teachers in both – it makes its point through the eerie comedy of Celeste's appearance at the school. Celeste is an angel, in every sense, and neatly set apart by the slight Victorian idiom of her speech. When she has come and gone, nothing is the same again.

Anne's trilogy of 'genie' stories, *A Sudden Puff of Glittering Smoke*, *A Sudden Swirl of Icy Wind*, and *A Sudden Glow of Gold*, are more exotic than her usual work, but even they are rooted in everyday school life (*Glittering Smoke*) and home life (*Glow of Gold*). *Press Play* is a story for the youngest readers, but the comedy of Mum's taped instructions for the morning pre-school routine shows the child just how much mothers usually do, and gently revisits the theme of sibling care for the youngest: Little Joe in his cot has his needs, too. And if children have needs, so do pets. In *Countdown*, Hugo James Macfie learns the hard way how lonesome the days might be for a neglected gerbil, and in *Care of Henry* Hugo finds out what the true priorities are when he can choose where to stay while his mother has a new baby, and the truest priority of all proves not to be Hugo himself, but Henry the dog.

At every level of readership Anne's stories are gently (sometimes toughly) educative and socialising experiences, and often they are acts of sympathetic therapy for the anxieties of childhood and adolescence. A small story like *The Haunting of Pip Parker* can be marvellous reassurance for the anguish of night-time fears. But they manage this while scarcely ever warranting the accusation of didacticism. Almost always they are comedies. And always, without exception, they are *novels* – not just stories, but narratives which introduce even the youngest children to the world of human choices, motives and feelings.

Peter Hollindale

1999

Bibliography

In date order

Books for older children

The Summer House Loon

Mammoth 1978

Ione lives with her father, a professor of history, and is a spectator to and meddler in the love affair between Caroline, her father's secretary, and Ned, a history student. As soon as Ione begins to make the most of the last few days of the holiday, chaos and confusion begin to spread . . .

Runner-up Kestrel/Guardian Competition 1975

The Other, Darker Ned

Mammoth 1979

In this sequel to *The Summer House Loon*, Ione's best friend Ned has married the scatty Caroline – will things ever be the same again?

The Stone Menagerie

Mammoth 1980

Ally thinks the weekly trips to see Aunt Chloe in the mental hospital are a waste of time, until he gets to know the people there. Then his whole attitude to life changes.

Round Behind The Ice-House

Puffin 1981

The twins, Tom and Cass, have always been inseparable. But Cass is changing, becoming more distant, growing up. Tom is disturbed to find himself excluded from her increasingly private life.

The Granny Project

Mammoth 1983

Four children work together to prevent their parents putting their beloved Granny in a home.

Shortlisted for Guardian Children's Fiction Award 1984

Playscript: Collins Education 1986

Madame Doubtfire

Puffin 1987

When Miranda advertises for a cleaning lady her ex-husband gets the job, disguised as Madame Doubtfire!

Shortlisted for the Whitbread Children's Novel Award 1987; runner-up for the Guardian Children's Fiction Award 1987; shortlisted for the Observer Teenage Fiction Prize 1987

Goggle-Eyes

Puffin 1989

Kitty hates Gerald and can't imagine what her mother sees in him.

Winner of the Guardian Children's Fiction Award 1990; winner of the Carnegie Medal 1990; shortlisted for the Smarties Award (9–11 section) 1990
USA: My War With Goggle-Eyes – *American Library Association Notable Book; International Reading Association Young Adult Choice for 1991; School Library Journal Best Book of the Year. Playscript: Heinemann Education 1995*

The Book of the Banshee

Puffin 1991

Will Flowers is very protective of his baby sister Muffy, who refuses to talk. With loving toughness, Will eventually cracks the problem. Meanwhile, Will's other sister Estelle inflicts her adolescence on the family with hilarious results.

Playscript: Collins Education 1995

Flour Babies

Puffin 1992

Simon and his class are given six-pound bags of flour to look after like real babies. Through this bizarre school science project, Simon learns about the strains of parenthood and begins to understand something of his own parents' behaviour.

Winner of the Carnegie Medal 1993; winner of the Whitbread Children's Novel Award 1993; Highly Commended, Sheffield Children's Book Award 1993; Birmingham TSB Children's Book Award, 1995. USA: Boston Globe/Horn Book Award Honour Book 1994; School Library Journal Best Book of 1994: American Library Association Notable Children's Book Playscript: Collins Education 1996

Step by Wicked Step

Puffin 1995

A group of children together on a school trip tell stories about their step-parents of one kind or another.

Shortlisted for the Sheffield Children's Book Award, 1996

The Tulip Touch

Puffin 1996

Not the least of Natalie's problems is the constant realisation that her younger brother Julius is her mother's favourite. However, this does not stop her fierce defence of poor, violent, cruel Tulip. But Natalie's friendship with the deeply disturbed Tulip leads her into dangerous ways.

Winner of the Whitbread Children's Book Award, 1997; Highly Commended, Carnegie Medal, 1997; shortlisted for the Sheffield Children's Book Award, 1997; Wirral Paperback of the Year, 1998. USA: American Library Association Notable Children's Book; Booklist Editor's Choice – 'Top of the List' Fiction; Bulletin, Blue Ribbon List, 1997; School Library Journal's 'Best Books of 97'; River Bank Review 'Children's Book of Distinction'. Playscript: Collins Education.

Very different

Mammoth 2001

Nine stories of teenage life, some funny, some serious, some both at once. James organises a pretend world tour for a garden gnome. Gregory must find a way to tell his parents he is gay. Antonia and her sisters face their spiteful, tyrannous

mother. Chloe's behaviour on holiday disappoints her
mother and grandmother, but not the Spanish waiter.
Teenage life is full of complications!

Up On Cloud Nine

Doubleday 2002

Ian's friend Stolly is in hospital, badly hurt after the
latest of many suspicious accidents. As Ian keeps watch
at Stolly's bedside, he writes down the story of their
friendship and works out a way to stop the brilliant,
unstable, sensitive Stolly from harming himself in
future misadventures.

Books for
middle children

Bill's New Frock

Mammoth 1989

Bill Simpson wakes up one morning
to find he's turned into a girl!
Winner of the Smarties Award (6–8

section) 1990; Highly Commended, Carnegie Medal 1990; winner of the Nottinghamshire Libraries Award 1990

Playscript: Longman Education 1992

The Country Pancake

Mammoth 1989

Lance comes up with the most original fund-raising idea ever – all made possible because of his friendship with Flossie the cow.

Playscript: Ginn 1997

A Sudden Puff of Glittering Smoke*

Mammoth 1989

Jeannie discovers a genie – and that means trouble!

A Sudden Swirl of Icy Wind*

Mammoth 1990

Banished to the storeroom, William accidentally

releases Mustapha, the genie of the bottle.

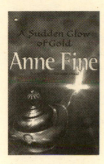

A Sudden Glow of Gold*

Mammoth 1991

Clearing out his room, Toby releases the genie from the lamp – and finally understands what wanting and needing really mean.

Anneli the Art Hater

Mammoth 1986

Anneli hates art until one day she finds a mysterious old picture and stumbles into a strange family drama.

Crummy Mummy and Me

Puffin 1988

Minna has a very unusual family, but at least it means life is never dull.

A Pack of Liars

Puffin 1988

Bored with her tedious penpal, Miranda, Laura takes on the identity of the imaginary Lady Melody Estelle Priscilla Hermione Irwin, and weaves a fantastic tissue of lies about her and her exotic life. But Laura soon learns that she's not the only one capable of deception.

Winner of Dillons/Puffin Birmingham Book Award 1991

The Angel of Nitshill Road

Mammoth 1991

Until the angel came, there were three terribly unhappy children at Nitshill Road Primary School. But after Celeste arrives, school will never be the same again.

Shortlisted for the Carnegie Medal 1993. Playscript: Ginn 1993

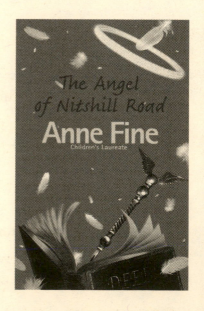

The Chicken Gave It To Me

Mammoth 1992

The story of a chicken who flies zillions of miles to try and save us humans . . .

How To Write Really Badly

Mammoth 1996

New boy Chester Howard sits next to Joe, the 'writer from Hell', and when Joe chooses 'How to Write Neatly' as his project, Chester persuades him to change the title to 'How to Write Really Badly'. So begins an astonishing partnership that brings rewards to both boys.

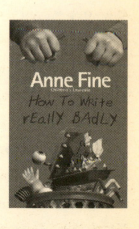

Winner of Nasen Special Educational Needs Book Award 1996; shortlisted for the Sheffield Children's Book Award 1997

Loudmouth Louis

Puffin 1998

A sponsored silence shows Louis how much nicer the world is without his constant chatter.

Prix Versele (Belgium) 2000

Charm School

Doubleday 1999

Bonny has no choice about going to the Charm School. If her mother is to keep her new job, Bonny must take this one-day class. Unfortunately, one day at Charm School turns out to be every bit as bad as Bonny feared.

Shortlisted for the Sheffield Children's Book Award 2000

Bad Dreams

Doubleday 2000; Corgi Yearling 2001

Melanie is a bookworm, happy enough at school provided she can stay in the library corner and not join in. Until new girl Imogen arrives, and Melanie is made her first-week minder. Imogen and her gold necklace bring real-life troubles into Melanie's safe world of books.

Shortlisted for the WHSmith Book Awards 2001; winner of the Stockport Schools' Book Award

Notso Hotso

Hamish Hamilton 2001

Anthony may be a mongrel dog, but he has high standards. When he develops a nasty skin problem, and the vet decides to shave him, Anthony is shocked. But life gets interesting, because Anthony's shaved and unshaved bits make him look like a lion!

Books for younger children

Design A Pram

Heinemann 1991

Poor Mr Oakway has to think of something to keep the class busy while he writes reports. 'Design a pram!' he tells them. Hetty and Oliver, the bossiest children in the class, take over straight away but they have very different ideas. So which design is the best?

Only A Show

Young Puffin 1990

What will Anna do for her five minute show at school?

Stranger Danger?

Young Puffin 1989

Joe learns his safety rules about speaking to strangers, but he soon realises that you have to use your common sense as well.

Playscript: Ginn 1994

Scaredy-Cat

Mammoth 1985

Everyone is looking forward to the annual Big School Horror Show. Everyone, that is, except Poppy. Ghosts and monsters terrify her and Poppy is determined to find a way of missing the show. But how can she prove to her classmates that she is not really a scaredy-cat?

The Worst Child I Ever Had

Young Puffin 1991

Susan Solly just loves snails! And that's one babysitter's reason why Susan's the worst child she ever had!

The Same Old Story Every Year

Young Puffin 1992

Mr Kelly and his class combine to put on a nativity play which is truly a triumph!

The Haunting of Pip Parker

Walker Books 1992

Something comes to haunt Pip Parker every night – but, of course, Pip's parents can't see a thing.

The Diary of a Killer Cat

Puffin 1994

The personal diary of a cat who finds himself in deep trouble after killing the nest-door neighbour's pet rabbit.

Winner of the Nottinghamshire Libraries Award, 1995; (FRANCE) Prix Sorcière, 1998; Prix de la Bibliotheque Nanterre; (BELGIUM) Prix Verselé

Press Play

Mammoth 1994

Nicky and Tasha find their mum has gone out but she's left them a note on top of the cassette player – 'Press Play'.

Countdown

Heinemann 1996

Hugo wants a gerbil, but Dad hates the idea of animals in cages. Can Hugo spend one day in an empty room to prove to Dad that it's not that bad?

Jennifer's Diary

Puffin 1996

Jennifer has no imagination. Iolanthe has zillions of

ideas for stories and nothing to write them in. How can she persuade Jennifer to hand over her diary?

Care of Henry

Walker Books 1996

Hugo has to choose who to stay with while his mother has a baby. Who will care for him – and his dog Henry – the best?

Roll Over Roly

Puffin 1999

Rupert and his unruly puppy, Roly, think Great-aunt Ada is the bossiest person ever – until they meet her parrot.

How to Cross the Road and Not Turn into a Pizza

Walker Books 2002

Simon is keener on maths than on learning road safety. So when Miss Talentino gives a practical lesson in crossing busy roads, she finds ways of turning Simon's maths to everybody's profit.

Jamie and Angus

Walker Books 2002

Jamie loves his new soft toy, an Aberdeen Angus bull called (naturally) Angus. Angus is never the same after Granny puts him in the washing machine instead of dry-cleaning him, but Jamie still loves him. Angus loves Jamie too, and is a reliable ally as Jamie tries to keep the difficult grown-ups in order.

Picture books

Poor Monty

Mammoth 1991

Monty's mother is a very busy doctor. When she manages to snatch a few moments rest after one hectic day, she finds that her own small son is not feeling well ...

Ruggles

Andersen Press 2001

Ruggles the dog loves his freedom. He is a veteran escaper from his owner's garden, all the year round. But now that he is getting older, perhaps winter is best enjoyed from indoors!

Anne Fine has also written five novels for adults.

The Killjoy, Black Swan 1986

Taking the Devil's Advice, Black Swan 1990

In Cold Domain, Black Swan 1994

Telling Liddy, Black Swan 1998

All Bones and Lies, Black Swan 2001

Anne Fine - Awards

1990 *British Book Awards Children's Author of the Year Award*

1993 *British Book Awards Children's Author of the Year Award*

1994 *Shortlisted for the BBA Children's Author of the Year Award*

The Ship of Theseus

Anne Fine

'Careers advice!' Mr Lang's lip curled. 'I'll give you careers advice! Find out what you like doing most in all the world, and then look for someone who'll pay you to do it.' And I thought how, by that way of judging, my dad's in the right job. He's a philosopher. I couldn't even say the word when I was little. It came out as 'flossifer' and I hadn't the faintest idea what it meant, except I assumed it had something to do with that peculiar white stringy stuff they kept next to the toothpaste.

Not that he didn't keep trying to explain. 'I *think*,' he said. 'That's what I do for a living. *Think*.'

Mum's got no time for it. '*Thinking*, you call it? *Arguing*, more like,' she always corrects him, if she's listening. Because he doesn't seem to do it very quietly. He's always thumping away about one thing or another, hoping that someone will pitch in and tell him he's wrong, so he can put them right about how he isn't. I'm like Mum. I act deaf – and stupid, too, if necessary – to get out of it. But Tabby listens.

Maybe she should be a philosopher too.

Strange thought. Because they're really weird, the things that it's his job to think about. Like when Tabs was little and splashing round in the bathtub while Dad was shaving, and she asked him suddenly, out of the blue: 'How do I know that all this round me isn't just a dream?'

He spun round so fast, so thrilled, he nicked himself quite badly. 'Look at her!' he called to Mum, blotting the blood from his chin. 'The philosopher's daughter! Four years old, and already an ontological sceptic!'

Whatever that is. And I must say, it does seem Tabby's far more on his wavelength than I am. I am forever walking into rooms to find the two of them wrangling away. Sometimes it's just normal family stuff, like her going on at him about finally finding the time to dismantle her stupid Squirrel's Night-time Hidey-hole halfway up the wall, so Mum can move in her new proper bed. (She is nearly *eleven*.) Or him grinding on about why tonight can't be the night they sleep under the stars. (She's been desperate to do this ever since I lent her *Oriole of the Outback*.) But Mum says she can only sleep outside if Dad is with her.

And he never gets round to it.

Too busy thinking.

This morning, it wasn't the bunk bed or the sleep-out. It was The Ship of Theseus.

Dad was explaining. 'So Theseus has this great big wooden ship, and everyone calls it The Ship of Theseus.'

'Makes sense,' I said. (I like to stick my oar in when I can – which isn't often.)

'And it gets more and more battered as time goes by – all his long voyages. So gradually, one by one, over the years, each single plank gets replaced. Every last one. And – this is the good bit – all the old planks just happen to float away in the very same direction, and fetch up, one by one, on the very same island.'

'Oh, very likely,' I scoffed. But Tabs was listening really hard.

'Now,' Dad said. 'On this island, it just so happens there's a master ship-builder, marooned for years. So he collects all the planks as they wash up on his beach, and one day, when he thinks he's got enough, sets to and builds himself a ship. And it so happens – pure coincidence, you understand – that every single rotting plank ends up in exactly its own place.'

He's grinning at Tabs now, and she's staring back, wide-eyed. It's obvious she can see something that I can't.

'*So*?' I say irritably.

Dad turns to me. 'What do you mean, "*So*?" It's only, put in a nutshell, one of the Great Central Questions of Western Philosophy!'

'What is?'

He stares at me as if I'm practically a halfwit. 'The *problem*, Perdita, is which is The Ship of Theseus?'

'Which?'

'Yes,' he says, trying to be patient. 'Is it the *old* one – I mean the one that's just been rebuilt from all the old planks? Or the new one that Theseus is sailing about in?'

I have to say, I take Mum's line on things like this. 'What does it matter?'

'What does it *matter*? Oh, it's only The Problem of Identity, isn't it?' He's clutching his hair now. 'Sweet heavens! It's only that awesome, overpowering question that's bothered some great philosophers their whole lives long: in what, exactly, is identity invested?' He's practically reeling round the room in his anguish.

Till he sees the look on Tabby's face.

She isn't even listening any more. She's lost in thought. Totally absorbed. Honestly, you'd think, to look at her, she could be Theseus on his firm new deck in a good wind, seeing, to his astonishment, a ship sail past, and wondering: 'Well, which one's mine? Neither? Both? This one? That one? But *why*? Perhaps that one first but, at a certain point, this one – or the other way round. But at which point? And why? Why? *Why*?'

The Philosopher's Daughter! So you can see why I spend so much of my Saturday out in the garden with Mum. We think that they're both daft. By coffee time, they were arguing about whether, if no one ever gets to see a particular tree in the middle of a forest, there's any way of being confident it's there at all. Then, later, as Tabs was setting the table for lunch, they reverted to the business of the sleep-out.

'Well, why can't we do it *tonight*?'

'Not tonight, Tabitha. I have a lot of work to get through tomorrow. I'll need a clear head and a good night's sleep.'

'You're always saying that.'

'It's always true.'

Mum poked at the risotto. 'Oh, not the sleep-out argument. Not again, *please*.'

(No point my offering to be with Tabs. All Mum ever says is 'Better one daughter murdered than two.' And even Dad daren't argue.)

Tabby moved back to the bed business. 'Well, why can't Dad at least take down my Squirrel Hidey-hole, so I can get my new bed in?'

'It's not as easy as it looks,' Dad said. 'That little bunk bed of yours is a complicated structure. It'll take time to dismantle it.'

Tabs slammed the last of the knives and forks and spoons down in their places. 'Bed? I'm so big now, it's practically a *cage*.'

'I'd take it down for you,' I offered, to try to help her make Dad feel guilty. 'Except that you've had to sleep in it so long that some of the screw heads are so badly rusted I can't get them started.'

'Don't think I haven't wasted hours of my own life trying,' Mum said, to pile it on.

'All right!' said Dad. 'I give in! Straight after lunch I'll loosen the screws enough for Perds and Tabs to take the thing down.'

'Hurrah!' said Mum. 'At last! And now could you two switch to arguing about something entirely different – especially not the sleep-out.'

I was only away for a moment, fetching the salad bowl. But when I came back, they were already launched. 'Now look, Tabs,' Dad was saying irritably. 'Do try and pay attention. It's quite simple.' Grabbing the knives and forks and spoons she'd only just set in place, he built a sort of track across the table, and then divided it at the end. 'There. See the fork?'

'Which fork?' Tabs asked him.

Dad stabbed the place where his line of knives and forks and spoons split into separate directions. 'This fork here.'

Tabs told him, baffled. 'That's a *spoon*.'

(Honestly, sometimes I reckon, when people think too hard, all the blood must rush away to warm up the clever bits and not leave enough to keep the basics – that's just common sense – working at all. Mum says that's why these really clever people are always hours late, or wandering around lost, or striding about with their woollies unravelling behind them.)

'What he means is the fork in his road,' I explained. 'Not a *fork* fork.'

Now Tabs was ratty. 'Well, he should have *said*.'

Dad was outraged. 'I did say! I explained right at the start. "This is the problem of The Angels at The Fork".'

'We're supposed to be eating with those,' I reminded them.

But, of course, neither of them was even listening. Sometimes you'd never think that Dad was thirty-seven and Tabs was eleven. You'd think they were both *three*, and busy squabbling in some sandpit.

'Ready to go on?' Dad asked Tabs, all sarcastically. 'Well, there are two angels standing by this fork. They look exactly the same. So do the roads. But one leads off to heaven, and the other to hell. And, though the angels are identical, one always tells the truth, and one always lies.'

'Always?'

'Always.' He beamed. 'And you, of course, want to get to heaven. But you can only ask one question. And all an angel can reply is "yes", or "no".'

'That's all?'

'That's all.' He spreads his hands in triumph. 'So, Tabitha, which question should you ask?'

He sat back, waiting. I would have said, 'You obviously know the answer. So you tell me.' But Tabs loves problems like these. Her forehead wrinkles up. Sometimes her fingers twitch as if she's working things through like a maths sum. Sometimes she stares into space. And sometimes she even mutters. I reckon if you saw her on a bus, thinking one through, you might easily reckon she was batty.

Even wrinkling and twitching and muttering didn't help her this time. It really stumped her, you could tell. She was still thinking about it even after Mum served up, and while she ate, and even while we washed up and Dad went to fetch the screwdriver and the oil to loosen the screws on her stupid little bunk bed.

She was still thinking as Dad pulled out the first screw. 'I could ask . . .' She broke off, shaking her head. 'No, that wouldn't work.'

'What?' I asked, holding the end up for Dad as he unscrewed the next bit.

'Well, I could ask . . .' Again she stopped, just as I

handed her the next strut. 'No, I couldn't. Because I might be talking to the angel who lies.'

'Couldn't ask what?'

She didn't hear me. She was miles away. She didn't even notice each time I handed her a piece of the bunk bed to put on the heap in the corner by the door. And Dad was so taken up with excitement of whether or not she'd get it right that he didn't notice he hadn't stopped working. He just kept handing me parts of the bunk bed, then got on with unscrewing the next bit.

Finally he couldn't bear it any longer.

'Give up?'

Neither could she.

'Yes. Give up.'

So, while I was stacking all the pieces of wood to take down to the bottom of the garden, he told her. 'You choose an angel, point up either of the roads, and ask the question: "If I were to ask the other angel if this is the road to heaven, would he say 'Yes'?"'

She thought about it. You could actually see her working her way through it. And then her face cleared and she beamed the same way he does. 'Brilliant! Excellent! That is so clever!'

I didn't mean to say it. It just popped out.

'I don't get it.'

Dad shook his head at me. 'That's because you're not *thinking*.'

Tabs turned to explain. 'You see, if the angel's answer is "no", then the road you're pointing along has to be the road to heaven. And if the angel answers "yes", it's the road to hell.'

'But how do you *know*?'

'It's obvious,' said Dad. 'It stands to reason, when you come to *think*.'

Tabby was kinder. 'Look,' she explained as we carried the bits of bunk bed down the garden path to stack them out of the way behind the apple-tree. 'Suppose you just happened to ask the honest angel. She'd truthfully tell you the other angel was going to lie, so "yes" would mean "no" and "no" would mean "yes".'

I managed to think that bit through, though my brain was practically *aching*.

Then, 'Go on,' I said.

'And,' she said, her eyes gleaming just like Dad's, 'if you had happened to ask the angel who tells lies, then she'd have definitely made out that the other would have given you the wrong answer.'

'Ye-es,' I said, still trying to catch up.

'So, just like before, "yes" would have meant "no", and "no" would have meant "yes",' she said triumphantly.

'Aren't angels *he*?' I asked, trying to keep my end up. But she'd dumped her last armful, and set off back to the house. So I just stood there a while, thinking about it.

And then I thought some more.

And that's how it turned out that, when Dad got exasperated with all the noise ('Tabs with her music on far too loud, and you with all that mysterious banging in the garden – you're driving me crazy. Please, can't the two of you just go off to your beds and read quietly or something?') we were as good as gold.

We came back twenty minutes later, ready for bed.

'Goodnight, Dad.'

'Goodnight, Perdita.'

'Night, Dad.'

'Goodnight, Tabs.'

She waited in the doorway, grinning. 'Well? Aren't you coming?'

He looked up, mystified. 'Coming where?'

'Down the garden for the sleep-out.' She spreads her hands, innocent as an angel at a fork. 'You know Mum says I'm not allowed to sleep out without you.'

'But we're not doing that tonight.'

'You suggested it. You only just said, can't we go off to our beds?'

His voice was heartfelt. 'Yes, indeed I did!'

'Right then,' she said. 'I'm only doing what you said. And my bed's outside.'

'Nonsense. I saw your mother and the two of you pushing it into your room.'

'No, no.' She winked at me – the genius who made all this possible, standing there inspecting the blisters on my thumbs. 'Perdita's put my Squirrel's Night-time Hidey-hole together again halfway up the apple-tree – every last plank in the same place. So, just like The Ship of Theseus, it's . . .'

She turned to me. After all, I'd done the work. I ought to be the one to crow it. 'Ta-*ra*! The Bed of Tabitha!'

Be fair. He knows when he's beaten, fair and square. He just trailed up to fetch his blankets and a candle or two, so he could keep working. In fact, I think he was delighted, really. Chuffed to bits.

There's more than one way of being a philosopher's daughter . . .